Pentecost Fire:

Preaching Community In Seasons Of Change

Gospel Sermons For Sundays After Pentecost (First Third)

Cycle A

Schuyler Rhodes

CSS Publishing Company, Inc., Lima, Ohio

PENTECOST FIRE:
PREACHING COMMUNITY IN SEASONS OF CHANGE

Copyright © 2001 by
CSS Publishing Company, Inc.
Lima, Ohio

All rights reserved. No part of this publication may be reproduced in any manner whatsoever without the prior permission of the publisher, except in the case of brief quotations embodied in critical articles and reviews. Inquiries should be addressed to: Permissions, CSS Publishing Company, Inc., P.O. Box 4503, Lima, Ohio 45802-4503.

Scripture quotations are from the *New Revised Standard Version of the Bible*, copyright 1989 by the Division of Christian Education of the National Council of the Churches of Christ in the USA. Used by permission.

Library of Congress Cataloging-in-Publication Data

Rhodes, Schuyler, 1953-
   Pentecost fire : preaching community in seasons of change : gospel sermons for Sundays after Pentecost (first third), cycle A / Schuyler Rhodes.
     p. cm.
   ISBN 0-7880-1824-8 (alk. paper)
   1. Pentecost season—Sermons. 2. Bible. N.T. Gospels—Sermons. I. Title.
BV4300.5 .R48 2001
252'.64—dc21   2001025097
                                                                                                 CIP

For more information about CSS Publishing Company resources, visit our website at www.csspub.com.

ISBN 0-7880-1824-8   PRINTED IN U.S.A.

*This book is dedicated
to the memory of my father,
The Reverend James Rhodes —
a perfect example of the
imperfect wonder of God's creatures.*

Thank you, Dad, for everything.

Table Of Contents

Foreword   7
    by Daniel Berrigan, SJ

Introduction   9

Pentecost   11
    Receiving The Holy Spirit
    John 20:19-23

Holy Trinity   17
    "I Am With You Always"
    Matthew 28:16-20

Proper 4   23
Pentecost 2
Ordinary Time 9
    Houses Built On Sand
    Matthew 7:21-29

Proper 5   27
Pentecost 3
Ordinary Time 10
    I Don't Need No Doctor
    Matthew 9:9-13, 18-26

Proper 6   31
Pentecost 4
Ordinary Time 11
    Sheep Without A Shepherd: Claiming Christian Leadership
    Matthew 9:35—10:8 (9-23)

Proper 7   37
Pentecost 5
Ordinary Time 12
    Disruptive Faith In An Organized World:
        The End Of Nice Christianity
    Matthew 10:24-39

Proper 8   43
Pentecost 6
Ordinary Time 13
    The Prophet's Reward
    Matthew 10:40-42

Proper 9   49
Pentecost 7
Ordinary Time 14
    A No-Win Situation
    Matthew 11:16-19, 25-30

Proper 10   55
Pentecost 8
Ordinary Time 15
    Good Seeds, Good Soil: The Call To Christian Community
    Matthew 13:1-9, 18-23

Proper 11   59
Pentecost 9
Ordinary Time 16
    Growing Together Until The Harvest
    Matthew 13:24-30, 36-43

Lectionary Preaching After Pentecost   63

Foreword

Religion concerns what we know about matters of heaven and of the heart. — Jacob Neusner

I have been exposed for more years than I dare recall to Pastor Schuyler and his "matters of heaven and the heart."

He and I were fated to become fast (in the sense of glue, not of speed) friends. I was invited to preach at his marriage with Lisa, an event precious and joyful indeed, for all parties concerned. They will never know.

Under the skilled tutelage of Schuyler and Lisa, Washington Square United Methodist burgeoned. At the start they tickled minnows; in time, they hooked dolphins. Denizens of the West Village in Manhattan, many of whom never dreamed so absurd a venture as darkening a church door, were intrigued. They came in.

Some truth (better, Someone) gained a hearing. The Sunday services were models of the welcome and inclusion that lie at the heart of the gospel. The arts, theatre, music, poetry, were taken seriously.

In this church, social concerns were not an addendum or footnote; they were the pith of what the church purports to stand for. War, poverty and homelessness, waste and want, the hand-in-hand of twin demons — you could enter Washington Square Methodist Sunday after Sunday and feel your heartbeat quickening; the bracing tang of truth, even the old-time thunderations of prime Methodism.

I came to admire Schuyler's sermons. Reading their text, I was struck by the rightness of the French saying, "La style, c'est l'homme." Something like this: "At depth, style bespeaks the person."

Put negatively, Schuyler doesn't pursue a way of writing or talking that 1) claims to speak for the gospel, and 2) seeks nonetheless to pull off a favorable hearing.

Such a weird conjunction of unlikelihoods (namely, that the gospel should conceivably be approved, hearkened, deemed of point, get itself sold or bought or integrated with the ethos of America) corresponds to nothing of reality, whether this be recorded in the original Acts of the Apostles — or for that matter in the Hebrew prophets, in Buddhism or Islam or Hinduism. Nothing in sum touching on the church's vocation at any point of history. Or today.

Rather, the attempt to adapt faith to the powers of this world, summons to mind the debased dream of this or that pudding-pated sycophant, playing clerical lap dog in the salons of the Blight House.

Nothing of this in the homilies of Schuyler, faithful as these are to the images and words and instructions, the dangers and ironies and pitfalls and pratfalls of the gospel. These sermons tell the truth, unsettling or devastating as they may be to conventional Christian ears.

The chips fall as they will, often wounding as they spin down.

Take care, woodsman, the ax of truth is razor sharp; so are the chips.

I love this little book. It weaves through our scripture with verve, dignity, and good humor; the touch is now light, now a flick of the whip, the words rife with the truth that hurts and heals, both.

Perhaps because the preacher himself has been hurt and healed, both?

Daniel Berrigan, SJ

Introduction

If we look to the state of our culture at the dawn of the twenty-first century, it's surprising that preaching has survived. In an age of sound bytes, streaming video, satellite television and more, the sermon and the one who delivers it stand almost as an anachronism. It is almost impossible to imagine that less than a century ago there were thousands of volumes of sermons published annually. In the nineteenth century the sermon was among the primary methods, not just of communication, but of literary form. The reasons, sociologically, politically, and religiously, could consume several doctoral theses. But for our purposes it is enough to know that both sermon and preacher are alive and well.

For Christian communities, the sermon continues to be almost sacramental in nature. At its best, it is a channel of God's grace; awakening, provoking, and offering a redemptive word in an unredeemed world. It is an amalgam of spiritual insight, communal perception, prophetic clarity, and pastoral care. The sermon is not mere entertainment, though one hopes for entertaining moments on Sunday morning. Neither is the sermon a lecture, though it is perhaps the pastor's optimum teaching opportunity. Finally, it needs to be said that the sermon is not a monologue, though it could easily appear to be so.

In contemporary Christian community, preachers are called to step into the pulpit to offer sermons that comfort and provoke; words that empower and offer vision. It is at once the most satisfying and frustrating work that falls to the busy ministry of any pastor. I daily alternate between shaking a fist at and giving humble thanks to God for placing me in the pulpit of a great and wonderful church.

This collection of sermons is a slice of church life. It is a cross-section of a pastor's vision and hopes. And it is a call to a people to claim their Pentecostal roots. Each of these sermons is predicated on the belief that the so-called mainline Protestant Church is not, in fact, in crisis. My own ministry and therefore my preaching rest on the unshakable belief that God is not done with the Church. In fact, we move and have our being in the assumption that God is doing a "new thing" in the life of the Church. We are claiming our Christian identity in new ways and building Christian community in some wonderful and powerful old ways.

These sermons reach for this new calling. They assume revival and hope in place of cynicism and despair. And they, along with the ministry I am privileged to share here in San Francisco, insist on new hope, new life, and new growth in Christ Jesus.

Pentecost
John 20:19-23

Receiving The Holy Spirit

Today is Pentecost. Today we celebrate the coming of the Holy Spirit upon the people of God. Today we celebrate the birthday of the Church of Jesus Christ, recalling our ancestors in the faith who received the power of God's Holy Spirit and began a journey which we continue in this moment as we take on the struggle to become a faithful people in today's world. Today we celebrate the arrival of the Advocate, the Spirit who accompanies and partners with us in life and faith.

That's a lot to say. And it's probably a good guess that many of the smiles in the pew this morning mask an interior monologue that goes something like this:

> *That's nice. But what is Pentecost? Where did it come from? What does it mean? Why do we even bother, on a nice weekend when most people are at the beach, to prepare special music and offer a special celebration? Who cares, anyway?*

Does this ring a bell? Would it be accurate to say that for some of you, this Pentecost thing is a little less than vague?

"This," said the preacher, rolling up his sleeves, "is what seminary professors would call a teaching moment."

The Greek word, *Pentecost* (Πεντεχοστ) is a word which traditionally refers to the fiftieth day after Easter. The traditional Anglican name for this is "Whitsunday." In pre-Christian days this holiday was an agricultural festival which scholars suggest gradually came to be identified as the festival time when the Jews celebrated the day that Moses received the Law from God on Mount Sinai. This being true, it then needs to be said that the arrival of the Holy Spirit and the birth of the new covenant community taking place on the same date that the Hebrew people received the seal of the old covenant is quite significant. I doubt that the coincidence escaped the understanding of the early Christian community. In fact, one of the articles I read suggested that Paul, in writing about the law and the spirit, was also lifting this up using a liturgical connection.

Today, however, *we* claim the celebration of Pentecost as a Christian event drawing primarily from the story described in the second chapter of Acts. There are ample other scriptural references to the Holy Spirit, of course. Today's lesson, for example, has Jesus breathing the Spirit on his disciples, telling them that they are called to forgive (John 20:22-24). In Psalm 104:24-34 we hear that we literally live and die according to the presence of God's Spirit. And I love the story of Moses and the elders (Numbers 11:26f) where people get peevish and jealous when one seems to have more "spirit" than the other. Moses cries out, "Are you jealous for my sake?" It's the old "grass is greener" syndrome. It's rather like those people who think pastors only work on Sundays. Or other folks who look at what you're doing and say, "Gosh, what an easy job. I wish I had that." You just grin and realize that they don't know what the job entails. Moses agrees. He says, "Are you sure you want this gift of prophecy?" "Would that all the people of the Lord were prophets and the Lord would put the Spirit upon them!"

Well, it took a while, but Moses got his wish. And it's this wholesale pouring out of God's Spirit that we celebrate today. It's the same thing that the writer of Acts repeats from the Prophet Joel:

> *I will pour out my Spirit on all flesh; your sons and your daughters shall prophesy, your old men shall dream dreams, and your young men shall see visions. Even on the male and female slaves, in those days I will pour out my spirit....*

It is from many and diverse locations that we arrive together in the Pentecost moment. This is an exciting time. The Spirit of God is upon us at Pentecost. It howls into our hearts like a mighty rushing wind. It dances on the heads of believers like tongues of fire, provoking them to dance and sing in such a way that onlookers think they are drunk. On Pentecost the Spirit is on the move, and we are all subject to its wonderful unpredictable rhythms.

But our focus today is on a different kind of Pentecostal moment. Today, through the window of John's Gospel, we pull back the sash and we don't see mighty winds or dancing flames. We don't see the Patriarchs arguing about who has more spirit. No. This is a different kind of spirit-moment. Through this window, we see a group of frightened, hunted men hiding out from the police. It is the rag-tag remnants of Jesus' followers who have gathered in this room in great fear and distress. It isn't a great time for the Disciples, as they were called. The leader has been arrested and executed, and most of the once robust group has scattered. And to add insult to injury, it was one of their own that betrayed Jesus in the first place! And now, we look, and see this dissipated and worn out group, gathered in this place of hiding.

What's next? What's left?

Who couldn't help wondering what fears and doubts were raging in their minds. Maybe they were in a kind of collective shock? It staggers the imagination. One wonders if they were even speaking to one another. Were they arguing and blaming? Did they sulk and weep? Were they planning next steps? Were they figuring on splitting up until things cooled down a bit? The Gospel of John gives us no details on this, but it's not hard to imagine some frightened, tired, and discouraged people huddling in a locked room while outside the police are looking for them. And suddenly, into the midst of this gloom appears Jesus. Into the smog of despair and defeat steps the Risen Christ, and he says, "Peace be with you." Peace be with you? Doesn't that seem like a strange thing to say? Here they are, hiding out and hunted; wanted men scared to death, and Jesus basically says, "Calm down." And then he breathes on them and says, "Receive the Holy Spirit. If you forgive the sins of any, they are forgiven. If you retain the sins of any, they are retained." Receive, in other words, the Holy Spirit of the Creating God, the power of forgiveness, the wonder of love, the hope of new life. Receive the accompaniment of God's power, a partner on the journey. Receive the power to forgive and the power to condemn.

This Pentecostal moment is a little more difficult than tongues of fire. It is a little tougher to get inside of than the hurricane of the Spirit that we experience in Acts. In the story of Pentecost in Acts, we have a faith community already gathered. There is momentum. People are coming together and celebrating the wonder of God in Jesus Christ, and *then* the Spirit comes upon them.

But here? This is different. Jesus marches into the sorrow of defeat and despair and offers God's wonderful Spirit. This is Jesus the gate crasher; Jesus crashing the party of hopelessness and gloom, telling his followers to relax, to calm down, and to receive the healing power of the Living God. This is Jesus, breathing hope into the midst of terror and defeat. This is the Spirit that moves forward into new life no matter what. It is the persistent solo voice of life, piercing the droning dirge of the choirs of death. It is, quite simply, the herald call of an unreasoning and unreasonable optimism in the worst of all possible times.

Most people don't like optimists. They usually are dismissed with a smirk and a quiet guffaw. Optimists. Give us a break. And when you consider it, there is some merit to the argument. Things in that room were desperate. Who knew what would happen? Arrest? Torture? Execution? They'd just seen it all. And then Jesus shows up and says, "Relax. I'm sending you out just like God sent me." And with that, the Disciples have to be thinking, "Sure, Jesus, send us out like God sent you. Look what happened to you! We'd rather stay put here until things cool down. Thanks, though ... It's, uh, good to see you."

Have you ever felt like the disciples must have felt on that day? Has defeat and exhaustion ever come to you so powerfully that you had to hide away? Have you ever felt fresh out of options? These are not times that we choose to jump up and down celebrating the wonder of God's Spirit. These are not times that we choose to reach out across the boundaries of our lives. And we seldom thank people who try to get us to do so. No. In times of defeat and despair, in moments of sorrow and pain, most of us are like the disciples. We find as safe a place as we can find, and we go in and lock the door. We hide, not really knowing, or thinking about next steps; not really planning or conniving. We just hide. It's instinct.

But, my friends, it is exactly into moments like these that Jesus insists on arriving. It is into Dietrich Bonhoeffer's cell in the days before his execution; it is into the dark nights of despair for prisoners of conscience; prisoners of fear; into our own dark places of regret and sorrow that Jesus simply appears, wounded hands in the air, saying, "Peace be with you."

It's really quite disturbing when you stop to think about it. "How did he get in here, anyway?" "We *thought* we were hidden pretty well." "We took the time to find a safe place, and to cover our tracks as we shut the door behind us." "We even locked the dead bolt." Like the disciples before us, we too lock the door as we hide away, trying to make sure that our isolation, our seclusion, is complete.

But the wonderful truth, the *Pentecostal truth*, is that Jesus doesn't need keys. He *is* the key! He doesn't need a map with arrows and directions pointing down the corridors and into the hidden rooms of our hearts. He doesn't need to know the way. He is the way! Jesus, already ever present in our lives, simply appears and stands among us saying, "Peace be with you."

He comes among us and shows us his wounds — not as an act of one-upmanship, for all of us bear wounds — but in a divine movement of solidarity. "You see?" he says. "I know how it feels. I've been there too. You don't have to be alone anymore." No matter where we're hiding, Jesus comes among us. No matter how numb we try to make ourselves, no matter how far we wander, Jesus comes among us. He comes and says, "You may be frightened. That's okay. You may be tired. That's okay. You may be discouraged or depressed. That's okay. It's all okay because the Holy Spirit is with you now." The wonderful Spirit of our God walks with you. And our God will ease your fears. Our God will lift you up and you will "mount with wings like eagles. You will run and not be weary, and you will walk and not faint" (Isaiah 40:31). And our God will sing you the song of new life so that you may dance in joy and celebration.

Today is Pentecost. And into this room comes Jesus, saying, "Peace be with you." Into our hearts comes Jesus, saying that just as he was sent by God, so are we sent by him to offer forgiveness and hope, new life and blessing. So whether the Spirit comes as a mighty wind with flame and power, or quietly into the fearful private places in our lives, rest assured, it does come. Whether the Spirit arrives in the voices and laughter of our children, or in the sorrowful faces of grieving loved ones, it does come. Whether it comes in a mighty wind of growth and movement, or in quiet healing ministries, the Holy Spirit comes and always comes among us.

We are blessed in abundance by God's Spirit, and the challenge that comes to us today is to open our hearts and our lives to the possibilities that the Holy Spirit offers. Who knows what wonders might be wrought, in our hearts, in our homes, our churches, even in our world, if we all embraced the power of God's Spirit in this time and in this place. Amen.

Holy Trinity
Matthew 28:16-20

"I Am With You Always"

Have you ever been hard at work on something? Perhaps you're like the pastor who sits laboring over a sermon or drafting a statement for this or that, or reading the latest biblical articles. Whatever it is, you are concentrating, focused, and suddenly you're aware that someone, somewhere is watching you. One day I was reading through a sheaf of mail in my office when suddenly I could just tell without even looking up that someone was peering though the curtained door to see what I was doing.

I don't know what made me aware of their presence. Usually it's not movement I see. It's something else. This person, mind you, wasn't trying to be nosy. She was simply trying to see if I was too busy to chat for a moment. But somehow I became aware that someone was there. Has that ever happened to you? It's as though some sort of sixth sense kicks in and you can *feel* the presence of someone close by.

One morning I was dozing peacefully in those moments before the alarm goes off ... and suddenly I had that same feeling ... like someone was there. Close by. I tried to convince myself that it was the hazy vestige of some dream I couldn't quite recall. But still that feeling was there. Of course this whole time my eyes were closed and I was more or less feigning sleep.

To myself I said, "Oh well, I might as well open my eyes to see who's out there." I opened my eyes, and there not two inches from my face were the blue, intent eyes of my three-year-old son. He blinked, and said, "Daddy sleeping?"

After peeling myself from the ceiling, it came to me that there was that feeling again. Even with eyes closed, it was clear that someone, somehow, was there. It is hard to describe as anything but a sense of presence. And for the life of me I cannot figure out what makes it work or not work.

Maybe this happens to you? I bring this up because today's Gospel passage has Jesus telling us that he will always be with us. We must acknowledge, I suppose, that we speak about people being with us like this quite a lot. My mother, before she died, said that she'd be with me. And sometimes, in a way much like that sense of presence, I do feel that she is still here. And I wonder if this sense of presence is the way that Jesus intended to be here.

Let's think about this. Here Jesus issues this "Great Commission" to us all. He says that "all authority" has been given to him. He instructs his followers to go and create disciples of all people, baptizing them in the name of God, the Word, and the Holy Spirit. And then he proceeds to instruct his followers — for our purposes, that's you and me — to teach these new disciples to obey the commandments that Jesus gave us.

It's funny here, one almost wonders if subconsciously Jesus knew how difficult a task he was laying on us, because almost like an afterthought he says, "And don't worry because I'll be with you always ... even to the end of the age."

It reminds me of my dad when he was teaching me to ride a two-wheel bike. I loved those training wheels. They were great. I could ride the big kids' bike and I never had to worry about falling down. Then one day I came out to get on my bike and my father had removed those training wheels. I panicked. Back into the house I went, whining and crying that I couldn't possibly ride the bike now. And my dad came outside and held the bike while I got on and said he'd hold onto it while I rode. "Cool," I thought, "as long as someone's holding on so I won't fall." Of course, two seconds later I looked back and he was at the other end of the driveway. I'd been riding on two wheels without him holding on and I didn't even know it. I am with you always, huh?

Now some might call this a hoax. Some might even look at this as a metaphor for a God who lets us think he or she is in control and then walks coolly off into the cosmos.

But I don't think so.

My dad wasn't holding on to the fender of my bike, but he was there. Not only was he there to pick me up if I fell, he was really and truly there. I could feel it. It was that presence thing. Even though he was a couple of hundred feet away, watching (I imagine) with some satisfaction, I *knew* he was there.

Jesus calls his followers to go out and create disciples. Hear that word, "create," because the translation of the scripture here is faulty. We are *not* to make disciples. We are not to coerce or judge, manipulate or threaten. We are to *create* them. As partners with God, we are to create disciples in much the same way that God created the world. And how did God do that? Out of love. We are to create new disciples with love. We are to grow them, to nourish and lift them up gently, fully, wholly. The days of whacking people over the head with a Bible as though you have some superior start in life are over. Nonetheless, though, the call is real and true. We are to go out there and create disciples.

And it has, at some point, to be asked: "How do you feel about your responsibility as an evangelist?" How do you feel about this part of being Christian? About the inescapable reality that as Christians, we are called to go out and preach the gospel to those who haven't heard it? How do you feel about your commitment to invite people, not just to come to church on Sunday, but to invite them into your life, into your community, into the transforming and healing love of God in Jesus Christ?

This could be off base, but it seems to me that people are uncomfortable about it. I would also guess that some people are uncomfortable even naming themselves publicly as a Christian, let alone inviting others to join us. Let me be honest. I've felt that. There have been times when I've seen an opportunity to offer Christ, to offer the life of this wonderful community to someone who could really use it ... and I didn't. Why? Oh, probably because I don't want to be associated with those television guys who cry alligator tears in front of the camera while stealing money from widows and orphans. I don't want to be identified with those religious men and women who prostitute themselves praying with presidents while giving their blessings to wars and horror. I don't want to be connected with a faith which is little more than a photo op.

Another reason is that I'm a good polite white liberal and I don't want to push my point of view too hard lest someone think I'm too aggressive.

What are your reasons? Why do you go through a whole week without asking someone to come to church? Why do you go through a whole week without telling someone about the love you've experienced through God's work in your church? Why do you go through a whole week without sharing the acceptance that you have gained in the love of Christ?

This is not an easy thing. Think about it. First of all, people don't like to be evangelized. They stoned Stephen, and they beat Paul and the others within an inch of their lives, then threw them into prison, not once but several times! This offering of love to the world is a risky business. People are so used to the pain and craziness of the world that they think it's normal, and anyone who suggests that it might be different, that there might be an alternative, is considered just a little crazy.

In fact, I know someone to whom I gave a gift subscription to a certain magazine. On the cover, it says something like, "A Magazine of Alternative Journalism." Now, this friend took one look at the word "alternative" and has refused steadfastly even to read the magazine, which comes to his house each month. He wants nothing to do with any alternative to the way things are.

Suffice it to say that there are lots of reasons why we might be a little shy about going out there. And we've only touched on a few.

But this is where this Jesus thing comes in. This is why Jesus said, "Don't worry, I'll be with you." Even until the end of the age. Even to the end of the age. Does that mean now? Absolutely. Jesus is with us. Now. Here. Wherever you are, Jesus is present. Real. You might become aware of it in the same way I sensed my son staring at me in my sleep. You may experience it like some unseen hand guiding you from down the driveway. Or you may encounter the presence of the living Christ in a totally different and unique way, which belongs to you only.

Or, you may have yet really to have that sense of presence.

Wherever you are in this spectrum of experience, I'm here to tell you it's real. I'm here to say that as we examine the challenge to share the love we have in God, we need to know that that love accompanies us as we go. Wherever you are, whomever you're talking to, whatever challenges or sorrows are visited upon your life, the power of the love of God in Jesus Christ is with you. This love isn't like some familiar and disingenuous peck on the cheek. This love isn't like the taste of a good pastry that is gone before the coffee gets cold.

This love stays.

It's presence walks with you, sits with you, holds you close, and bids you share it. And the operative word here is "share." Our call to evangelism is not a call to arrogance. It is a summons to humility and gentleness. We are called to move forward, offering Christ, not in bluster with trappings of worldly power, but in true surrender to the ways of love.

This is necessary for our own integrity. It is also necessary because of the people we will meet. The un-churched, the un-faithed, the atheists who march about announcing that they don't believe in God, these are the folks with whom we will be speaking. And the underlying truth, in my experience, is that most of the alleged atheists I meet are not atheists at all. In fact, most of them haven't really given a lot of consideration to notions about or experiences of God. What they don't believe in is the Church! What they reject is the heavy-handed, irrelevant rantings of our institution. And I say BRAVO! It's not the church we're called to believe in! We're called to believe — to trust — in God's love as it has been brought to us in Jesus Christ. Yet many of us who try to meet the challenge of inviting others into the love of God shy away not because of this, but because of what the Church has done.

Once and for all, let's today say loud and clearly that the Church is a broken and sinful structure. We are called to be very mistrustful of sinful structures. Let's move forward, past what the Church has done about evangelism and claim anew the Great Commission. Let's reject the old ways of manipulation and coercion, the evangelism of guilt, shame, and threats. And let's cast upon the waters new bread, new hope, new offers of gentleness and love.

Let's offer the Christ we know in open, loving Christian community. The one who accepts us all as we are, and calls us into community and solidarity, who challenges us to embrace ministries of justice and compassion, who holds us close and walks with us every inch of the way, even unto the cross, if that is our path.

So I challenge you. I invite you. I encourage you. I double dare you: "Go, and create disciples of all nations, baptizing them in the name of the Creator, the Word, and the Holy Spirit, and teaching them about the love of God in Jesus Christ." And don't worry, because Jesus will be with you always as you do this ... even unto the end of the age. Amen.

**Proper 4
Pentecost 2
Ordinary Time 9
Matthew 7:21-29**

Houses Built On Sand

One evening the television news was filled with stories about home-owners on the west coast whose multi-million dollar homes were slipping slowly, but surely, into the Pacific Ocean. Grief-stricken faces crowded the screen, calling on the local government to come and do something. Some even tried to get the State of California to intervene as their houses inched downward in a slow, steady dance toward the sea.

It's hard not to have sympathy for someone losing his or her home. We place a lot of ourselves in the buildings in which we live; no one wants to see anyone out on the street. But there's something about this scenario that unsettles my insides. Stuck in the mind's eye are the camera shots of houses slightly askew with the Pacific Ocean in the background, beckoning. For the most part, these folks paid serious dollars for their homes. Many people, myself included, dream about a home overlooking the ocean. The land on which these houses stand — or stood — cost more than the houses most of us live in today.

And yet, they build their houses, quite literally, on the sand. It doesn't take a rocket scientist to drive around these neighborhoods and predict that sooner or later these folks are going to lose their front lawns, then their driveways, and ultimately their whole houses to the inexorable march of the tides. Yet still they build. Even today as we sit here they build. On hurricane alley in North and South Carolina, they build. In the Gulf of Mexico, on coastal plains where floods and hurricanes are normal occurrences, they build.

And then it happens. A house falls into the sea. A condo is swept off by hurricane winds; a cottage evaporates in gale force winds. We've heard it all before. Yet the next thing that happens is rebuilding: new houses on the sand ready for the next storm to come and sweep them away.

It's very interesting to note that few of Jesus' illustrations in the Gospels carry such vivid and direct application to our world today. If we stop to consider it, things don't get much simpler. If we hear God's word and don't act on it, we only need to look at coastal real estate to get a graphic picture of what our lives will look like when the storm comes.

If, on the other hand, we receive God's word and act on it, then the story is different. Then we will be like the person who built his house on the rock, and the winds and the storms came and whipped and lashed to no avail. For the homeowner had built on a firm foundation.

It all seems so simple. The illustrations are crystalline in their clarity, and the direction forward could not be more bluntly stated.

We don't get just to talk about our religion. We don't have the luxury of merely going to church on Sunday for an hour so we can hear the preacher give us some moral pick-me-ups for the week ahead. No, we are to *hear* God's word, and then to act on it.

This scripture issues a challenge to the Church as it has been, and to the Church as it is called to be. The Church of today is really a house built on sand. It is a shaky proposition, a rickety structure laid out on the shifting sands of doctrine and ideology. It is a wilting collection of folks — all well meaning — but all gathered in the pews to hear the word without acting on it; without actually letting it touch and transform our lives.

Yes, some will disagree and point to all the good things that the Church does. True. There is much to applaud in terms of charity and comfortable shelter from the storms of a society which teeters between dysfunctionality and insanity. But the Church of Jesus Christ was not called forth by the Holy Spirit to be a sheltering place. The Church of Jesus Christ was born of the Spirit and nourished by the Word. And if we only sit idly by and listen to that Word without being touched, without being transformed, without turning and acting on what that Word calls us to do, then we are indeed resting on the quick-sand of our own inaction.

Today the so-called mainline churches of American Protestantism stand at a critical junction in their history. The situation is tense. Membership is down. Vision is blurred. Mission is unfocused. We have become a people who hear the Word but do not act on it. And the waves are lapping at the front steps of our houses built on sand while we busily restructure and quarrel over demonic tidbits of doctrine.

Fortunes have been made by scores of writers with greeting card theology, simple solutions, and structural realignments. We can pretend the Church is a business and follow a business plan. We can de-structure and let people follow their passion. Or we can swerve dangerously into neo-orthodoxy, snuffing out the vital intellectual quest that a living faith requires.

Or we can be hearers and doers of the Word.

We can, if we choose, quit all the noise and begin to do the gospel. Saint Francis is quoted somewhere as challenging his followers to "preach the gospel at all times, and when necessary, use words...." We would do well at the beginning of this century to heed the call of the little monk of Assisi. We have an opportunity before us to renew, remake, and revive the Church in ways that we cannot even imagine.

If Christian folk were found in the urban trenches, feeding, healing, housing, and loving in Jesus' name; if Christian folk were found in the prisons and the migrant camps offering advocacy, education, and hope in Jesus' name; if Christian folk were found singing their hearts out in solidarity on the picket lines where laborers are exploited and workers endangered; if they offered solid support and succor in Jesus' name; if Christian folk were found dismantling the weapons of war in Jesus' name; if Christian folk were found in all these places, sisters and brothers, a revival would explode as never before. If Christian folk were found placing their bodies on the line in Jesus' name, the Church would not be slithering away into irrelevancy, nor would it be wasting its time fighting over meaningless points of doctrine. For we would be both hearers *and* doers of the Word. We would be living out our faith in God through Jesus Christ our Lord!

And, friends, the world would respond to that.

And we, the Church, would have begun to build our house on the solid rock of lives lived faithfully in Jesus' name. We would be not only hearers, but doers of the Word. Would we be perfect? No. Mistakes would come as surely as the dawning sun, as surely as they do now when we only sit idly by and listen. Would we be free from conflict? No. But conflict, we might learn in our struggle to live the Word, is a healthy part of our being together in community and ministry.

Sisters and brothers in Christ, the gospel challenges us today to be both hearers and doers of the Word. Will we accept the challenge? Will we embrace Jesus' call? The answer belongs to us all.

**Proper 5
Pentecost 3
Ordinary Time 10
Matthew 9:9-13, 18-26**

I Don't Need No Doctor

There's an old rock and roll song titled, "I Don't Need No Doctor." The song, like so many of the era, is a song of unrequited love. The lyric, screamed out by a number of rock bands over the years, says, "I don't need no doctor, 'cause I know what's ailing me." And what's ailing the singer, of course, is the deprivation of the object of his affection. He is smitten, out of control in the painful, bittersweet carnival ride of adolescent love. "I don't need no doctor, 'cause I know what's ailing me." I remember many years ago swaying to the sounds of this song at a very loud outdoor concert. But I must confess, I didn't think about the words very much. I don't think many of us did. I just wanted to feel the rhythm and dance to the music.

But now, in reading the Gospel of Matthew, this song returns to me. I even pulled out my scratched and faded vinyl LP by a British band named Humble Pie, and played through it a few times. Each time as I listened to the surging rock beat and the simplistic lyric, I couldn't help reflecting on this passage. Some of you may want to question this, I know. But as we read through the Gospel and hear Jesus responding to his critics, it's interesting to consider.

In this passage, Jesus is sitting, as he often does, with a host of marginalized and outcast people. We are not really certain who these people are. Scripture doesn't get too specific about their sins, except to name the tax collector Matthew. The others are simply "sinners." We can but guess at the list of wrongs committed by the others, but it seems clear that tax collectors were chief among sinners. I hope no one here works for the IRS.

The scene is spread out before us in a wonderful tableau. Jesus is at table sharing fellowship with these tax collectors and sinners. They are eating, drinking, talking, laughing, and sharing. As so often happens, critics line up to take pot shots. In this scene, however, they don't even try to confront Jesus directly. They approach his followers, trying to initiate a kind of smear campaign. "What does he think he's doing?" they ask. "Why is he sitting with them? Doesn't he know that *they* aren't the kind of people a self-respecting Messiah ought to be seen with?" The stage is set, once again, for the somewhat inept disciples to try to interpret the often-mystifying behavior of their Teacher.

After all, they are good Jews. They know the implication of sitting with a man who extorts taxes to support the occupation forces of Rome. And what about those other sinners? Let's take an educated guess. I'll bet there were some unclean and non-Jewish folks sitting with him that day. There may also have been a prostitute or two. And certainly he would have welcomed women to his table. It chills the soul of any good, pious Jew of the first century.

But Jesus is eavesdropping. Were you brought up to envision a Savior who eavesdrops? I wasn't.

But there he is, head cocked and listening in like Aunt Minnie through the bedroom door. He hears them and responds with a powerful sense of irony. "Those who are well have no need of a physician." One can almost envision the scene. These people are gathered, upright and pious, preening just a bit as they take in the words of Jesus. He is, they think, absolutely correct. "We don't need no doctor. *They*, on the other hand, need ... something. *They're* sick. Even Jesus says so...." But Jesus has a follow-up to his often-quoted retort, and cuts short their self-congratulations. He dismisses the good, pious religious folk, and tells them to go and figure out the meaning of these words: "I desire mercy and not sacrifice, for I have come to call, not the righteous, but sinners."

Remember that these are the people who truly believe that they "don't need no doctor." They are religious authorities. They are the Holy Ones who think they have it all down. These are the people who find Jesus troubling, even threatening because he is

— to say the least — unorthodox. It is these people that Jesus flippantly sends back to school. "Go and learn what this means."

And it is here that the admittedly shallow lyric of the old rock song comes alive. It's an arrogant stance at best. "I don't need no doctor, for I know what's ailing me." I've got it together. I know what's going on. I have a problem, and you're it. In fact, if you'd only cooperate, there wouldn't *be* a problem. For the adolescent love-lorn pining for the object of his — or her — affection, it's a passing phase (we hope). But for the good, pious religious folk who cannot abide Jesus and his world-changing love, it is a mantra. For those who believe it is their calling to cement and codify religious belief into the bonds of creed and doctrine, it is a balm in Gilead. We don't need no doctor; we know what's going on here. We don't need no doctor; we only need you to fall in line. We don't need no doctor; we need all you who are different than we are to get lost. We don't need no doctor; we got a lock on God, on Holy Scripture, and on what's right and what's wrong, and you'd better listen.

The guardians of orthodoxy and right belief, both then and now, sing on in frightening harmony. "We don't need no doctor, for we know what's ailing us ... and it's you, Jesus, with your insistence on disobeying our rules. It's you with the company you keep; it's you with your cavalier attitude toward our laws." And the song continues today as the arbiters of religious correctness wail on: "We don't need no doctor, 'cause we know what's ailing us ... and it's you, gays and lesbians; it's you, tree huggers and environmental activists; it's you, human rights advocates; and it's you, who would open the doors of our faith to *anyone* who wants to come in...."

But Jesus, his eyes twinkling and his spirit soaring through the ages, sits at table with his friends, and sends those who think they are well back to school. "Go and learn what this means," says Jesus. "I desire mercy and not sacrifice." The Greek word for mercy here is *elios*, meaning kindness. "Go and learn what this means," says Jesus. "I desire kindness and not sacrifice. I desire kindness and not exclusion. I desire kindness and not narrow legalism. I desire kindness and not smug self-righteousness. I desire kindness and the willingness to open your hearts to all my children."

So it is that that old rock and roll lyric picks up the gospel and follows us today. "I don't need no doctor, 'cause I know what's ailing me." It shouts down the years to those who think they know. It pounds on the doors of our institutions and their need to control. It dances into our consciousness and calls us to question our own smugness and self-righteousness. And it pours over us with the power of God's Holy Spirit saying that, in truth, we don't need no doctor except Doctor Jesus.

And so let us all go back to school. Let each one, in the grace that God offers, learn anew that God desires kindness and not sacrifice. Let us come together across the chasms of our differences and build a gospel bridge of hope and understanding. Let us join together in ministry as we set a table where everyone, sinners of all stripes and colors, even tax collectors and pastors, deacons and bishops, are welcome. In Jesus' name. Amen.

**Proper 6
Pentecost 4
Ordinary Time 11
Matthew 9:35—10:8 (9-23)**

Sheep Without A Shepherd: Claiming Christian Leadership

My sister is a chronic room re-arranger. Her beautiful home in upstate New York seems always to be in a state of change or rearrangement. She's a gifted artist, and enjoys the task, which always results in stunning rooms and creative living spaces. But the family joke is that we know when she has something on her mind because there will be a new arrangement of furniture in her living room or den. It's not an uncommon thing. Many people with concerns or issues on their minds will find ways to occupy themselves while they work out things in their minds. It's good. It's healthy. It serves a purpose.

But not all rearranging is helpful. Sometimes we move to change things because we sense despair and failure, and we think that moving the furniture will drive the dark of doom away. It brings to mind a scene I remember from a scratchy black and white film made in the early 1960s. Air raid sirens have signaled an impending nuclear attack, and there in her kitchen is a woman preparing a pan of lasagna for the evening supper. Deliberate, focused, careful. What else could she do?

A similar scenario is playing itself out among our churches. It seems that the last decade has wrought an epidemic of restructuring within our mainline Protestant churches. If one listens, the sounds of moving furniture can be heard across the landscape. Everywhere there is deconstruction, reconstruction, and rearrangement. From the Lutherans to the Presbyterians to the United Methodists, with a few more in between, and back again, the furniture is being moved. Process Teams, Task Forces and all manner of well-meaning groups are coming up with a myriad of organizational options in the vain hope that structural change will stop the hemorrhage of membership, resources, and vision that most communities are now experiencing.

> *Then Jesus went about all the cities and villages, teaching in their synagogues, and proclaiming the good news of the kingdom, and curing every disease and every sickness. When he saw the crowds, he had compassion for them because they were harassed and helpless, like sheep without a shepherd.*

As we gaze at our institutional church life and watch what is happening, this passage offers a powerful message. It shows us a Jesus on the road; a Jesus engaged in the ministry of healing and hope; a Jesus busied with preaching the Good News. There is, in the economy of language used to describe it, a wonderful sense of energy and enthusiasm about the work that Jesus is doing in the "cities and villages." He has traveled far and wide teaching in the synagogues, preaching to the people, healing their illnesses, and curing what the Gospel refers to as "every sickness."

And it is as though somehow in the midst of the wonderful work, Jesus stopped and took a break. And while he was knocking back a diet cola, he couldn't help noticing how tired and dispirited the people seemed. It was hard to miss the fact that they were "harassed and helpless ... like sheep without a shepherd." So Jesus sits down, one imagines, and sighs. He turns to his disciples and he says, "See? The harvest is plentiful, but the laborers are few; therefore ask the Lord of the harvest to send out more laborers...."

To hear about the activity and power of Jesus' ministry on the road is inspiring indeed. It comes full force as a challenge and a call to us all. But then we need to stop, with Jesus, and notice that our people, too, are harassed and helpless, like sheep without a shepherd.

They are harassed by a culture gone mad with the pursuit of wealth and material gain. They are tormented by a society that has put a price tag on everything and everyone, rendering all things into commodities. They are distracted by a Church that is more concerned with the exigencies of institutional survival than with living out the gospel of God in Christ Jesus. And they are helpless, or rather, feel helpless to do anything about it.

And understand this. Our people, our good Christian folk, are not helpless in the sense that they cannot or will not act. They are not helpless in the sense that they are weak and without resolve. No. They *feel* helpless because they — because we — need visionary and bold leadership, and there is none. "And where," scripture tells us, "there is no vision, the people perish."

We in the Church need to confront the truth that real, authentic leadership has been abandoned for soft tissue concepts like "enabling" and "empowering." Faith communities have been left to drift, fracture, or simply dissipate while concepts and styles of leadership fill seminary classrooms without producing leaders. The articulation of clear vision and powerful motivation has given way to consensus and caution. Leaders are taught in seminaries and leadership workshops across the nation to "delegate" their authority, and to let the people lead. All of these, of course, are wonderful and excellent ideas that are appropriate in community process. But they do not, they cannot, replace the role of leadership.

In the midst of the frantic pace of reorganization and restructuring in our churches, there is an unspoken truth illustrated by today's Gospel passage.

We do not need restructuring. We need leadership.

It's a flip and unhelpful thing to say, perhaps. But even Jesus could see that people needed leadership. Even he stepped and filled a leadership gap, because they were "sheep without a shepherd."

We need leaders in the Church. We need leaders who have clarity of vision and a sense of passion for the gospel. We need leaders who are not tired or weary, burnt out or cynical. We need leaders who love the Lord and their people. We need people in leadership positions who are not afraid of failure or of risk. We do not need perfection or adherence to doctrine or orthodox principles. We need Spirit-filled powerful leaders who will inspire and provoke our people to do great and wonderful things in Jesus' name.

Sisters and brothers, we don't need restructuring. We don't need Strategic Planning or Quest for Quality. We don't need reorganization.

We need leadership.

The sheep, my friends, need shepherds! The harvest is plentiful! The membership of our churches may be waning, but there is a spiritual hunger out there, which is near famine proportions. Inside our churches, inside this church, we are blessed with incredible gifts in our layfolk who are straining at the leash to be led into ministries of healing and evangelism; tasks of feeding the hungry and bringing justice to the oppressed. Our folk are prayerful and good people, and they need shepherds.

Now it needs to be said in all the excitement, that leadership isn't dictatorship. Leadership isn't for people with control and power issues. No. And leadership isn't about one style of leadership or another. The best leaders understand a wide variety of styles and approaches to ministry, and pray for the wisdom to know which is needed. Leadership is the ability to lift up a people to new heights, to call forth their gifts in new and powerful ways, to articulate a vision that includes and touches everyone. No, we don't need the old style bosses. We need prophetic, pastoral caring leaders in our pulpits, in our council seats, and in our bishops' chairs.

Jesus points out that the people are like sheep without a shepherd. A shepherd in Jesus' day had an interesting job. By day he made sure that there was grass for the flock to feed upon and that predators were kept at bay. Every night the shepherd would make a crude wall or corral out of sticks and brush, and before he would let the sheep inside, he would walk over every inch of the enclosure, making sure that scorpions, snakes, and other dangers were removed. Then he would bring the sheep in for a night of rest and safety.

Not only do our churches need leaders who are bold and prophetic, but also we need leaders who will work to create safe places for Christian community to grow and thrive. Each person walking into one of our churches must feel welcome and safe. Each person must be placed at ease, able to open one's heart to what we have to offer in the gospel and in community. In this ease and safety, these same people must be challenged to go deeper into their faith, deeper into discipleship.

The ministry to which we are all called is a powerful and world-transforming task. It is a gift of a wonderful God. Let us not squander this incredible gift in a haze of institutional reorganization. Let us not force our people to jump through ever smaller hoops of doctrine and ideology. Please, dear Savior, free us so that we might lift up new shepherds for your sheep, new leaders for your people, new visions for your Church. In Jesus' name. Amen.

**Proper 7
Pentecost 5
Ordinary Time 12
Matthew 10:24-39**

Disruptive Faith In An Organized World: The End Of Nice Christianity

Once, not too long ago, a certain pastor was leaving the grocery store with some supplies for his family's evening meal. Outside in the parking lot he noticed a woman in her car trying to back out of a narrow spot. Pastor set his bag down on the pavement and got the woman's attention by waving and waving. He then proceeded with dramatic arm gestures and directions to assist the woman in backing her car out of the spot. Feeling quite smug and self-satisfied for his good deed he picked up his bag and strode over to the car where the woman had opened her window and was motioning to him. He leaned down into the car about to introduce himself and the woman said, "Friend, that was thoughtful and all, but the truth is that I was trying to get *in* to that parking space, not out of it.

It seems like there are times in life when we arrive on the scene, thinking we know what's going on around us. We arrive, clear in our minds that this situation is well in hand and we're just the ones to take charge and manage it. And then cruel reality steps in and disabuses us of any illusions we may have had. We find, in fact, that not only are we out of touch with what's happening, we may even have gone and stepped on someone's toes or otherwise upset the apple cart, because — in truth — we were clueless.

Can anyone here identify with being clueless? New parents often feel clueless. You would think these babies would come with instruction booklets. But they don't. And clueless parents stumble on, relying, if they're lucky, on family who have been down that road before.

It seems to me that the gospel is often addressing a clueless people. We wander about doing our level best to be good Christians doing the thing that's right — or at least expedient. We wander about, working hard, giving our time, talents, and resources to build what we think is a nice, pleasant Christian community: a good place, where people don't argue, where everyone likes everyone else, and where there are always enough people to do what needs to be done.

Isn't that what we all kind of keep in our minds? Whether we admit it or not, isn't that the ideal? And isn't a great deal of our disappointment and disillusionment based on the truth that we never really realize this ideal?

So many times we hear about people who storm out of our churches because there was an argument over the budget or a disagreement about the pre-school. Listen carefully and you can hear the disdainful tones. "Yeah! They call themselves Christians, and you should have seen them arguing!" Or, shocked at politics in the religious community, similar voices register their disapproval. "Churches? Right. They're supposed to be Christian, but once you get in there, it's all politics. Have you ever been to one of their meetings?"

It's difficult to escape this pervasive myth of so-called nice people in so-called nice Christian communities trying to live up to this very strange expectation of being so nice. Where, one has to wonder, does this come from?

It's safe to say that it doesn't come from our Gospel reading for this morning. Because most pastors are just as invested in so-called nice Christianity as you are, this morning's Gospel reading is one we like to avoid. It ranks up there with preaching about divorce and, even worse, peace. Most of us, if we were truthful, would just as soon leave this out of the Bible, or at least the lectionary.

But there it is, staring us balefully in the face. Our lovable, gentle, huggable Jesus has the audacity to stand there and tell us that he didn't come to bring peace, but a sword! What are we supposed to do with this? What are we supposed to do with a Jesus who tells us that he has come to set people against one another? Is this the Jesus that you have come to know? Is this the Jesus with whom you want a "personal relationship"? This Jesus says he wants to break up families! He wants to "set a man against his father, a daughter against her mother, and a daughter in-law against her mother-in-law"! Is this a Jesus that supports "family values"?

This is all very troubling. Not only does this Jesus want to break the peace and smash families, he also says that if we love our parents more than him we're not worthy of him.

It's easy to see why a lot of folks would just rather pass over this scripture.

Yet as we come together in faith to grow and to move forward in ministry, it's important — perhaps even critical — that we be certain not to miss this piece of scripture. You see, this scripture is rather like an iceberg floating in the cold north Atlantic, and our pervasive myth of a nice guy Jesus and nice fluffy Christianity are like the *Titanic*. We think our big, lumbering ocean liner can't sink. We believe that our gentle, loving Jesus works very well for us. But in order for this myth, this one-sided, one-dimensional Jesus, to work, we must ignore this and other scriptures.

The quick and oft-heard response to this is that Jesus is actually condoning violence and military action. I have heard it said by otherwise sensitive and intelligent persons that this is a portrayal of the "realistic Jesus," and it is to be played off against or balanced with the Jesus who calls us to love our enemies.

Let's set the record straight. *Jesus does not condone violence or military action, anywhere in scripture.* Furthermore, any attempt to justify such sinful behavior with scripture is a violation of the spirit and the letter of God's new covenant with us in Christ Jesus.

So, we have that out of the way.

What, then, is going on here? What could possibly explain this invasion into an otherwise acceptable picture of Jesus as the quintessential nice guy? Could it be that Jesus is not trying to say that he's here to bring war and disruption, but is instead describing what will befall us if we are faithful in following his teachings?

Think about it.

If we truly followed the teachings of the Master, what would happen to us? If we gave away our material goods to the poor, if we brought homeless men and women into our own homes, if we actually made an effort to love our enemies and to pray for those who abused us, if we really worked at living out these teachings, what would happen?

The scenario begins to gain some clarity. The picture clears up, and it begins to make sense. For those who truly and authentically follow the teachings of Jesus of Nazareth, it will be as though he had come with a sword. Imagine your family's reaction if you sold everything you own and went to live in poverty with a Franciscan order? I doubt such behavior would be met with overwhelming approval. Imagine if your family came home to find fifteen or twenty homeless people laid out in sleeping bags in the den and living room? Imagine if you invited your dad's worst enemy — the one from the office — over for dinner? It would be easy to continue this list. But it seems clear.

Contrary to what some Christians would have you believe, following the Christian life is not a ticket to well-being and prosperity. In fact, it's quite the reverse. If you truly fulfill the "royal way" (James 2), if you give your life over to following the teachings of Jesus Christ and what early Christians called "the Way," there will be discord and division. It is likely that your family will be at least unhappy. And you can rest assured that you — like our Lord and Savior before us — will be labeled as a troublemaker.

Now that we have crossed this bridge and gotten in touch with some of the consequences of faithful living, the inevitable question arises. What will we do? Will we slip comfortably back into nice guy Jesus? Will we return to our cocoon churches that turn away from conflict and unpleasantness? Will we continue to hide away in a Church that — in all honesty — resembles a religious social club more than a community of Christians redeemed by God's love in Christ? What will we do?

Whatever we do, let us not return to business as usual. Whatever we do, let us not live any longer in the past. Whatever we do, let it flow from an open commitment to the teachings of our Lord and Savior. Whatever we do, sisters and brothers, let it be a bold and courageous step forward on our journey into faithfulness.

What will we do?

Maybe we'll take one step into faithfulness and move our ministry into caring for hungry and homeless sisters and brothers. Maybe instead of a faceless "them," we will discover women, children, and men with life stories, with hopes and dreams, with much to offer us and our community. If we open our doors and invite hungry people in to be fed, if we place cots around so that homeless people have a warm, safe place to sleep, we will surely incur the displeasure of some. But we will just as surely be taking a step on the path of faithful witness to the love of God in Jesus Christ.

What will we do?

The question remains to be answered by each of us and by all of us. But today is the day that we must say together that the question can no longer go unanswered. Today is the day we begin to give birth to new vision and new hope. Today is the day that we will lift up the ministry of our God till it shines forth in wholeness and healing. Today is the day we begin again in God's love to build, to strive, to grow, and to move in faithfulness.

Whatever we do, sisters and brothers, let it be done in faithfulness, in wonder, and in joy. Whatever we do, let us do it loudly, proudly, and boldly in Jesus' name. Amen.

**Proper 8
Pentecost 6
Ordinary Time 13
Matthew 10:40-42**

The Prophet's Reward

Children are sometimes the best teachers one can imagine having. At six, my son has figured out that behavior unbecoming of him has consequences. He has also figured out that behavior above and beyond the call of duty can have certain rewards. A bedroom cleaned extra well or dishes unexpectedly cleared from the table and washed can have a reward of sorts. The reward could be an extra half-hour of television beyond the allotted hour per day. It might be a walk with Dad to the ice cream parlor on the corner for a double dip cone. Or it might simply be an affectionate hug and a "thanks for the good job." But whatever it is, he has learned that there are rewards for good behavior.

This is the way of the world, isn't it? At our jobs, in our families, and in our other relationships, we generally function on this notion of actions and consequences. It's a system, if you will, of rewards and punishments. It seems crude, almost cruel, to put this way, but there it is. While unfairness and injustice surely exist and while exceptions can certainly be raised, it is safe to say that if we work hard and perform well on our jobs, things generally go well for us. If we focus on our families, giving them the love and attention they deserve; if we are intentional about treating our spouses, our children, and our siblings well, then things — most of the time — tend to go well.

We have learned to expect this, and in our social context have codified both the rewards and the punishments. Pay scales are usually tied to performance evaluations and length of service. Even pastors understand that a series of churches served well will lead to bigger churches and hence larger paychecks. On the other hand, the post office regularly hosts series of photos displayed prominently where everyone can see them. The rewards here are abundantly clear.

Rewards and punishments. They punctuate our lives and walk with us through most of our days. Each of us can relate stories of ways in which we have felt rewarded in our lives. A friend who is partial to jigsaw puzzles feels rewarded when a large puzzle is completed. A pastor in a nearby town works on restoring antique cars as a hobby and feels rewarded when he completes work on an old Model A pick-up truck. Some people involved in the ministry of the church feel rewarded when they participate in visitation ministries or when they give a day to Habitat for Humanity.

For us, the notion of reward has taken on a sense that it is something extra. We get a reward if we have done something a little special. A reward is over and above what usually takes place for us. A reward is given for exceptional work or behavior. But as we think about the notion of reward as it relates to scripture, we need to reshape our thinking. Chapter 10 of Matthew, our text for this morning, speaks of reward.

> *"Whoever welcomes a prophet in the name of a prophet will receive a prophet's reward; and whoever welcomes a righteous person in the name of a righteous person will receive the reward of the righteous; and whoever gives even a cup of cold water to one of these little ones in the name of a disciple — truly I tell you, none of these will lose their reward."*

This passage is our focus for today, but in truth, the Gospel of Matthew seems keen on the notion of reward. It's mentioned eleven times from chapter 5 through chapter 10 of Matthew. We are offered all kinds of ideas about reward. "Rejoice and be glad for your reward is in heaven ..." (5:12). "If you love only those who love you, what reward do you have?" (5:46). "Don't practice your piety before others in order to be seen by them; for then you have no reward from your Father in heaven" (6:1). "Whenever you give alms don't blow a trumpet before you as the hypocrites do in the synagogues and in the streets so that they can be praised by the others. Truly I tell you, they have received their reward" (6:2).

It's interesting to note that through all of this, the Greek word *misthos* (μιστηοσ), which actually refers to a wage or amount paid for hire, is used consistently. So the reward that we wish to explore today is not the kind of reward we see in the post office, though some prophets seem to attract that kind of thing. It's not necessarily something above and beyond — something extra — for our troubles. It is, instead, understood as the wage paid, the recompense for work completed.

This being so, what are we to think about the prophet's reward? What are we to think about welcoming a prophet or a righteous person — or even a disciple of Jesus Christ? What is it that we are paid? What is our wage? Our recompense if we welcome one of these into our homes or our communities? Are we expecting a wage? Do we wish or want to be recompensed for offering welcome? What is the normal pay? That's what most people would ask. "What's union scale for a Prophet's welcome?"

More than thirty years ago, Jesuit priest Daniel Berrigan and his brother Phillip participated with seven other people in the burning of draft records in Catonsville, Maryland. This was a prophetic act. The people who did this were prophets speaking God's truth about a horrible war being waged a half a world away. As a result of this and other actions, and for reasons we won't go into today, Father Dan, as his students often called him, decided not to turn himself in to the authorities, and went, instead, underground. For quite a while Father Dan led the FBI and other federal agents on a merry chase. For months this prophet of God was welcomed by scores of people. They fed him, housed him, drove him to meeting spots. Finally, after months of being "on the lam," Father Dan was arrested at the home of a close friend. He then spent an extended time in Danbury Prison.

The prophet's reward.

Were all the people who gave Father Berrigan refuge sent to prison? Did they receive the prophet's reward? No. But quite honestly, it wasn't because the FBI didn't wish it so. Indeed, had

J. Edgar Hoover had his way, they would have all been locked away as enemies of the state.

It's a challenging concept to engage, and an interesting thing to consider.

And as we do so, let us have a degree of clarity. We *are* called to welcome the prophet and the righteous among us. We *are* called to open the doors to disciples of Jesus Christ. We *are* expected to offer hospitality, in fact, as a basic tenet of who we are as Christians. There's no way around it. It is our calling. It is our commitment. It is, as people of faith, our responsibility.

But what, we ask, is our reward? What, to render it into an accurate portrayal of the Greek, is the payback? And, perhaps more uncomfortably for us, are we willing to go there?

If a young man in the military was about to embark for duty and discovered that he couldn't in Christian conscience kill a fellow human being, would you welcome him? Hide him? Give him refuge? And if so, what would be your reward? If a righteous person, an activist struggling for workers' rights, sought refuge from the authorities in your home, would you offer a place to stay? Would you prepare a meal? Would you offer clean clothing and transportation? Think of all those who sheltered the thousands of people who resisted apartheid in South Africa. Think of those who gave shelter to workers in the American Underground Railroad. Consider those who have sheltered refugees, illegal aliens running from violent and corrupt governments in Latin America. What is to be their reward? What would be our reward if we actually took the risk of this kind of hospitality? The answer should be abundantly clear.

Finally, we must address the third person in this interesting Trinity. Would we receive a disciple of Jesus Christ? It's a powerful testimony to notice that a Christian disciple is mentioned in the same verse as a prophet and a righteous person. Are we to infer from this that Christian disciples should be prophetic and righteous? Are we to assume from this that it is a Christian duty to struggle for peace and social justice? To wage a righteous struggle for what is right and good in the world? Are we actually to take it upon ourselves to offer aid and sustenance to those who have committed their lives to this kind of work, this type of ministry?

In seminary they say that preachers aren't supposed to give the answers. A good preacher poses the questions and leaves the congregation to ponder the answers. But friends, today an answer accompanies the questions.

It is absolutely and unavoidably the duty, the responsibility, and the privilege of every Christian to engage in the struggle for social justice and peace. It is the calling of a justice-loving God that each disciple of Jesus Christ be a prophet and a righteous person. We are in all of our moments as individuals and community and in each of our days as faithful followers of Christ to welcome the prophet, to welcome the righteous, and with them in solidarity to pursue the building of a world of hope and new life, a kingdom where God's peace and equity will reign.

And, yes, we can expect the prophet's reward. We can expect the ire of the powerful and the anger of those who are "in charge." But we can also expect the joy and wonder that accompany those who risk God's justice and love. We can reap the rewards of those who walk toward healing and wholeness in the world, a reward of knowing that you — in this moment — are doing what is right and good in the presence of your God.

This is the prophet's reward. This is the cold cup of water, the loving touch, the breath of a wonderful Savior. Amen.

**Proper 9
Pentecost 7
Ordinary Time 14
Matthew 11:16-19, 25-30**

A No-Win Situation

I think one of the best lessons I have learned in ministry is the lesson of win-win. Have you ever heard of win-win? In a world where win-lose situations seem to dominate our interactions, the discovery of the possibility of building scenarios where everyone can benefit, where everyone can, in effect, win, has been an incredible answer to prayer. In church, community, and family life it has been a powerful way forward on numerous occasions. Recently, an experience in negotiations in a sensitive church situation resulted in a win-win, and it was unbelievable. Former adversaries threatening to leave the church walked out of the room as friends with renewed commitment to the faith community. Those who were once miles apart on some serious issues found themselves looking to common ground and seeking common language. It was a thing of beauty, a moment of grace.

It's a good bet that most of us have been in a win or lose situation. Some, too, have had the blessing of a win-win outcome. But almost certainly, everyone has encountered a no-win situation.

A no-win situation is just one of those times, one of those moments, when no matter where you turn or what you decide, the outcome isn't going to be as good as you had hoped. Sometimes, in fact, it seems that no matter what you do, the outcome will be just plain bad. It's like the story about the young fellow coming home from school who took a side street to avoid bumping into this girl. As he turned the corner, he suddenly found himself confronted by the school bully. What to do? Face a certain beating, or turn and face the girl who made him stutter and blush? Definitely a no-win situation. In another instance, a friend was offered a speaking engagement at a distant university. His children were young and he really didn't want to be away from his family. Neither, however, did he wish to disappoint these folks with a negative answer. So, thinking himself rather smart, he called the university and said he couldn't possibly accept the speaking engagement for less than $6,000, which was more than three times his usual fee. Without hesitation, the voice on the other side of the phone accepted his offer. No-win. Either he leaves his family for a week, or charges more than he knows ethically he should for his services. No-win.

Don't you just hate no-win situations? Perhaps the good news is that everyone seems to experience them at one time or another. Former President Clinton, after hearing from a number of citizens about the lack of United States aid to a beleaguered African country, changed his mind and worked to ensure that country the aid it needed. Suddenly, his critics were sounding off that he was inconsistent, because he changed his mind. No-win. From presidents to pastors to teachers and back again, everyone finds oneself at some point in a no-win situation. It just seems to be the stuff of life.

Even Jesus had the problem. For him, the problem centered around meeting — or not meeting — peoples' expectations. None of us, of course, have that problem. We can hear the tension that Jesus had to confront as we explore this Gospel passage. One can sense his frustration, as he compares the people to a group of children who are never quite satisfied:

> *"To what shall I compare this generation? It is like children sitting in the marketplaces and calling to one another, 'We played the flute for you and you did not dance; we wailed and you did not mourn.'"*

Who among us has not heard the whiny, complaining voices of children who simply are not satisfied by anything. The conundrum is clear. And Jesus gets the point home as he relates it to his own situation.

> *"For John came neither eating nor drinking, and they say, 'He has a demon'; the Son of Man came eating and drinking, and they say, 'Look, a glutton and a drunkard, a friend of tax collectors and sinners!'"*

Jesus' cousin John was an esthete. He dressed in rough clothes and lived a spartan life. Jesus, on the other hand, loved life. He ate, drank, and spent generous amounts of time at table with friend and foe alike.

They were both equally criticized. No-win.

Jesus says, "Look at my cousin John. He was a real hermit, eating nothing but grasshoppers and honey. You didn't like him much, did you? Well, I'm nothing like that. I sit down and eat a good meal. I love to be with people and celebrate, and you call me a drunk. I just can't win with you people!"

Poor Jesus. It does seem like he couldn't win, doesn't it? Do you think his no-win situations were similar to ours? Do you think that we all fall into these things from time to time? Or do you think perhaps Jesus had an extra strike against him? Interesting.

Win-win. Win-lose. Lose-lose.

Winning and losing is quite important to us, isn't it?

In fact, it's more than "quite important." Winning or losing is really about how the game is played. Some might say that winning or losing is the game. I once saw a bumper sticker that was trying to be funny, but it stated the reality. "It's not how you play the game that matters. It's whether you win or lose." Losing, you see, isn't an option. At least it's not an option if you want to be valued, to be taken seriously, to be considered a real person.

Olympic athletes trying out in most countries work over a series of trials to see if they can get on the team. But in the United States there is one chance, one shot only. You win or you lose. You're on the team, or you're not. You can train for years and years to get on this team, and if you have a bad day — too bad. You lose.

And Jesus stands at the intersection of our obsession with the game, our insistence on lining everyone up and making them into winners or losers, and challenges us. Jesus, who found himself in the ultimate lose-lose situation calls to us, waving his arms with the children in the square. "To what shall I compare this generation?" I think the truth is that he can't think of anything that compares with us. We are singular in our need to have losers and winners. We, like the critics to whom Jesus is responding, wouldn't like John the Baptist or Jesus. Both of them were losers: one beheaded, the other crucified. Losers.

But still, Jesus calls us, o'er the tumult of competitive lives and says it is, in fact, about how we play the game. Win, lose, or draw, it doesn't matter. Having the most toys, the biggest car, the nicest job, the fanciest church? None of it matters at all. It doesn't matter if you wear camel's hair, eat locusts and honey, and run around baptizing. It doesn't matter if you sit at table with the marginalized and the outcast. The question has to do with faithfulness.

Win-win situations are, of course, wonderful. And as a pastor my hand goes up to vote for that. But the truth is win-win can't always happen. Sometimes "no" is the answer, and there is no way to let everyone win. Sometimes you're the one who loses, and sometimes everyone loses. There really isn't a lot of control that you or I have over things like that. What we can control, though, is our own faithfulness to that which we know is right.

We know it's right to love and lift up others. We know it's right to share the glory. We know it's right to err on the side of compassion and justice. And we know it's right to put right action before victory.

Jesus knew this too. That's why he compared himself to John the Baptist and said, "You didn't like John and you don't like me." He was saying, in effect, that they — that we — won't like anyone who doesn't play by the rules.

So they both lost. Or did they? Was Dorothy Day a loser? Was Mahatma Gandhi a loser? Was Martin Luther King, Jr., a loser? All the women and men who have given their lives nonviolently for love — were they losers? No. For, as Paul writes in his letter to the Church in Rome, "we are *more* than conquerors through him who loved us" (Romans 8:37). We are better than winners because we have rejected the very idea of winners and losers. We are more than conquerors because we would rather do what is right than win.

No wonder people grow frustrated with Christians. No wonder, too, that Jesus observed wryly that he was in a no-win situation.

But, sisters and brothers, we are not in a no-win situation because we're losing. We are in a no-win situation because we have risen up together to claim victory beyond winning. We have joined arms and hearts to claim that the struggle is over and the battle is done, and the winner is not you or me; it isn't the kid who used to wait after school to beat you up; it isn't the boss who called you a loser. No. The winner in every battle is our wonderful God who has won the victory in Christ Jesus.

As we go forward in ministry to grow and reclaim our Church, let us abandon the notion of winning. Let us ask for God's strength to help us let go of our need for success, and to ask only for the strength to be faithful to God and to God's Living Word, Jesus Christ.

Win, lose, or draw — it finally doesn't matter. Camel hair and grasshoppers or wine and good company. Win-win, win-lose, no-win. All we need to seek is faithfulness to our calling, to our community, and to our common heart in God's love. Amen.

**Proper 10
Pentecost 8
Ordinary Time 15
Matthew 13:1-9, 18-23**

Good Seeds, Good Soil:
The Call To Christian Community

Not too long ago I was in a garden shop and I bought a "meadow in a can." Have you ever seen one? It's a rather clever form of marketing. The would-be gardener has only to purchase a can about the size of a large frozen orange juice can. But it's not frozen and there's no orange juice in it. Inside the can is a huge variety of wild flower seeds. The idea is that the would-be gardener is to spread these seeds over an unsuspecting meadow. Then all that is needed is the waiting, while the stretch of lawn is transformed into a riot of color, a magazine cover example of beauty and grace.

Well, the can of seeds came home and was spread judiciously around the meadow. We waited. And waited. We waited one year, and nothing happened. Then we waited two, and three, and finally on the fourth year a goodly number of wild flowers appeared in the field. It was really quite beautiful. The names and groupings escape me now, but it was quite impressive. I turned to my dad and said, "Did our little meadow in a can do that?" He looked at me and smiled, and shook his head as he headed back into the barn. It wasn't until later that I learned that seeds very likely wouldn't last four years out in the open, and that the appearance of the wild flowers in that field was God's own wonderful action in wind and the movement of all things.

I had obtained something which our parable doesn't cover. Bad seed. We had, or so I was certain, excellent soil. No rocks or thorns, no thorns or thistles, just good soil. But those seeds. They were a bad lot.

In a world such as ours, so little is certain. We stand this morning with the sower, watching seed spill out on all manner of landscapes, only, as the parable tells so well, to see them baked, choked, or cut down in their prime. Occasionally, some land on good soil, and a harvest of plenty proceeds. But sometimes, even when luck is with you and the good soil is targeted, you find that you've got bad seed. Sometimes even the unlikely chance of defeating the odds and finding good soil won't save you, because you bought "meadow in a can."

And once in a great while, in spite of all the barriers and problems, good seed finds good soil, and amazing things happen. Sometimes the fit is just right. Sometimes the harvest is amazing.

In seminary, we were told never to tell our congregations what the seeds represented. We were warned never to try to assign identity — metaphorical or otherwise — to the thorns or rocks or shallow soil. Instead, we were challenged to let the parable tease the hearer, to tell them as Jesus did by letting those who have ears hear the power of what is being offered in the story.

None of us really liked this idea. In fact, we wondered if Jesus had really said, "Let anyone with ears, listen." After all, these stories beg to have values assigned to them, don't they? It's almost impossible to avoid telling you who I think the shallow soil turns out to be. It's all I can do to keep from blurting out certain politicians' names when I hear about the seeds being choked by the thorns. And the birds, eating up all the seeds? Have I ever got a few ideas on that one! And then there's the place that Jesus didn't even go! What if, what if the seed itself wasn't viable! Hmmmm. What if this seed wasn't going to grow no matter where it landed? Do you have any ideas about that seed? Do you have any notions of what it might represent?

Don't you see why we rebelled against interpretation in seminary? Do you see how hard it is simply to let the story speak?

It is indeed difficult. But that is precisely what Jesus called his people to do. And it is what we are called to do if we wish to enter the beauty and grace of the parables. When we hear a parable today, the last thing we need to do is to begin assigning values and names to the things we wish to be symbolic.

Parables were a kind of teaching story used by many rabbis in Jesus' day. This seminarian was quite surprised to find out that Jesus didn't invent them himself. But they were commonly used, not as symbolic moral tales, but as creative stories designed to invite the hearer into the world of the story — the world of God's Kingdom. The people of Jesus' day would have understood the idea of a sower tossing seeds all around the place. That, quite simply, is how farming was done in those days. A farmer would walk about casting seeds as he went, and then come back later to harvest what had grown up. And indeed, the seeds did land in a multitude of locations, with only a fraction of them ever producing fruit.

Fine. No potent symbolism, no hidden political meaning; just the story and — what is it that Jesus says? "The ears to hear"?

So it falls to us to ask today, who were the people listening to Jesus? What was the context of their being? What truths could be revealed by Jesus sharing what to most of them was an obvious story. They knew, after all, how seeds were sown. They also surely knew about the randomness of their falling, and the resulting harvest or lack thereof. What do you think they heard? What truth did the early Christian community uncover from these simple, powerful stories?

What do *you* hear? What, in this style of first century agriculture, in this random tossing of seeds and occasional growth and harvest, do you hear? Where does this speak to your life? How does it speak to the community of faithful? What is it we hear in this parable as we sit down together to plan for ministry, to engage in "making disciples of Jesus Christ" (Matthew 28:19)? How can we mine the gold of Jesus' parables without attaching our own agendas and twenty-first century issues to his stories? How can we gain the ears to hear?

A first step might be for us to come clean about our issues, about the values and symbols that pop into our heads as we read a parable like this. It's likely that a conversation about this would be very revealing indeed. And as we share all of our pieces of applied meaning and agenda, we just might begin to empty ourselves. We just might begin to share a bit about the people to whom Jesus was talking. We might, in abandoning our issues, be able to enter the world of the people who originally heard these stories.

And as we go deeper, we might become aware of the struggles of the early Christian community; aware of how this story might have truly touched and spoken to them. Then, perhaps we might have ears to hear. Then perhaps we might touch some of the wonder of the Kingdom that Jesus shared in these powerful stories.

Or we might try to tell the story in a way that we could understand. We might take the familiar pieces of our life and fashion them into a story that would speak truth to us in a new and different way. How would you tell it? Maybe we could give this a try.

One day a computer programmer took a new program to the university to download into all the computers in the classroom. And as he went along downloading the software, some of the computers were not compatible, and were unable to read the program. Others had hard drives that were crashed. Still others could receive the software, but when a user tried to run it, the whole system would crash. And then there were a few computers that accepted the program perfectly. The software ran well and allowed the students to do a great many things in their studies.

If you have ears, hear. Amen.

**Proper 11
Pentecost 9
Ordinary Time 16
Matthew 13:24-30, 36-43**

Growing Together
Until The Harvest

I once knew this person who had both the blessing and the curse of utter clarity in his life. This person knew — or at least believed with all his heart that he knew — what was right, and what was wrong. Subsequently, he also knew — or at least believed with all his heart that he knew — which people were right and which were wrong. And by extension, this young man also knew — or at least believed with all his heart that he knew — which people were good and which people were bad.

He was a marvel of simple alacrity. He could make decisions with a snap of the fingers. He could even, with fatally flawed logic, argue almost anyone to a stand-still. And he could easily select the people with whom he wished to spend his leisure time. Until, that is, his job forced him to move to a place where almost everyone and everything fit his description of "bad." Suddenly, almost as though directed by a God with a sense of humor, this young man was plopped down in the midst of a neighborhood, into the middle of a community that — according to his understanding and clarity — was bad. The streets were dirty. The people were loud. And the children ran incessantly up and down the sidewalks, causing all manner of racket. There was no telling what was going on behind those doors. No telling indeed.

This guy was really upset. What good is clarity if it's muddied by your surroundings? He really thought he couldn't hack it anymore. Finally, he decided to ask his boss for a move, and if his boss wouldn't grant it, he would just have to take his chances and quit. Enough was enough.

There he was, fuming. There he was, rehearsing his speech to his boss, when all of a sudden that ill-behaved gang of kids came rattling down the sidewalk. One of the leaders among them stepped forward and said, "Hey, mister, we think we found your wallet down the street. Here." The man's mouth dropped open. For indeed there was his wallet. He did have the presence of mind to wait until the children had turned and headed back down the sidewalk. But then he quickly checked. Yes. All the cash was there.

Only moments later a group of friends were sitting there at the scene of the crime that didn't happen, and this person was asked about his transfer request. His answer was this. "If I leave now I might miss a chance to turn those kids around. I guess I can hang in here until the next move comes."

And the parable that Jesus relates in Matthew 13:24-30 tells of weeds that have been planted by an enemy in the midst of good seed. Terrible weeds, deceitfully planted in the dead of night by someone bent on weakening the crops that were promised by the good seeds. It turns out of course that the weeds cannot be pulled without also uprooting the wheat. And so, we let them grow together until the harvest.

Interesting stories, don't you think?

Isn't it interesting how enemies creep in and adulterate the good seed with weeds? Isn't it interesting how someone can get dropped into a field which seems to be weeds, only to learn that maybe this is the prime harvest? Isn't it interesting?

It's important, it seems to me, to acknowledge the multi-faceted truth presented here in these stories. Our gentleman who was blessed, or cursed, with clarity knew — or believed with all his heart that he knew — about good and bad. And he knew — or believed with all his heart that he knew — that he didn't want to be around the things that were bad — until he didn't have a choice.

Now let's get real. Who among us wishes to spend time in the midst of people they don't like? Who chooses to go into situations where they will feel uncomfortable? And who, once forced into the situation, can find even the grudging fortitude to stick it out and harvest a goodness they didn't even know existed? This guy's okay.

And consider for a moment, the farmer whose field has been seeded with weeds by an enemy. The weeds have taken root and cannot be removed without removing the very thing the farmer is trying to grow. So he shrugs and says, "Let them grow together until the harvest."

"Let them grow together until the harvest." Let them be together like our gentleman in the neighborhood he so despised. Let them grow and intertwine with one another until the harvest when the weeds will be collected, tied together, and burned.

In one case we tolerate that which we cannot abide, and as soon as the first opportunity arises, we rip it out and destroy it. Now, for the Christian community of Matthew's time, this story had some specific meaning. There were many different sects, and many different teachers were offering a host of different ideas — weeds if you will — among the good seed.

I know, I know. Last week we said not to attach values or symbols. But this is really a little more than that. The question that comes to us as a contemporary Christian community is how we deal with weeds. Do we let them grow together and then root them out at the harvest? Or do we find ourselves in a field of diversity and difference, and decide grudgingly to hang out for a bit to see what's going on?

Today, sisters and brothers, these questions are before us in much the same way as they confronted the early Church. How do we deal with weeds? How do we confront differences of doctrine and opinion? How do we encounter divergent ideas and teachings? Are we sitting patiently by, waiting to root out that which is different? Are we taking note of the weeds and marking them for the burning? For the Christian community of Matthew's day, that may have been needed. But I wonder if new times might be calling us to new fields and new methods of farming.

Could it be that we might — in today's Church — be a little more like my friend? Could we, in today's Christian community, be in a place where we might need to hang out and see what's going on before we bolt? Before we pull out the weeds and burn them?

What do you think?

Do we live in a world where insisting that Jesus Christ is the only Lord and Savior for all people for all time is a good thing? Can we live in a world where Jesus Christ is *our* Lord and Savior? A world where the love of God in Christ Jesus is real for us, and in a world where Mohammed may speak God's voice to Islam as well?

Are we a people who simply tolerate the differences among us, waiting for a chance to stamp them out? Or are we a people secure in the love of our God, and able to learn from other people's experience of what is holy?

These are big questions; enormous challenges. And some people would wish that they were not upon us. Some people would sit patiently counting the weeds and awaiting the harvest. But I wonder, in faith, if that is truly our call in the twenty-first century. I wonder if, in truth, we are called to wrestle with diversities of faith and doctrine. I wonder if we are called to embrace the struggle of how to live in a shrinking world where people have authentic experiences of God that just might be different and valid.

Can we grow together until the harvest? Can we intertwine our roots? Can we hang around and see what a different neighborhood has to offer? In the love of God in Jesus Christ, let us pray that this is possible. Amen.

Lectionary Preaching After Pentecost

The following index will aid the user of this book in matching the correct Sunday with the appropriate text during Pentecost. All texts in this book are from the series for the Gospel Reading, Revised Common Lectionary. (Note that the ELCA division of Lutheranism is now following the Revised Common Lectionary.) The Lutheran designations indicate days comparable to Sundays on which Revised Common Lectionary Propers or Ordinary Time designations are used.

(Fixed dates do not pertain to Lutheran Lectionary)

Fixed Date Lectionaries *Revised Common (including ELCA)* *and Roman Catholic*	Lutheran Lectionary *Lutheran*
The Day of Pentecost	The Day of Pentecost
The Holy Trinity	The Holy Trinity
May 29-June 4 — Proper 4, Ordinary Time 9	Pentecost 2
June 5-11 — Proper 5, Ordinary Time 10	Pentecost 3
June 12-18 — Proper 6, Ordinary Time 11	Pentecost 4
June 19-25 — Proper 7, Ordinary Time 12	Pentecost 5
June 26-July 2 — Proper 8, Ordinary Time 13	Pentecost 6
July 3-9 — Proper 9, Ordinary Time 14	Pentecost 7
July 10-16 — Proper 10, Ordinary Time 15	Pentecost 8
July 17-23 — Proper 11, Ordinary Time 16	Pentecost 9
July 24-30 — Proper 12, Ordinary Time 17	Pentecost 10
July 31-Aug. 6 — Proper 13, Ordinary Time 18	Pentecost 11
Aug. 7-13 — Proper 14, Ordinary Time 19	Pentecost 12
Aug. 14-20 — Proper 15, Ordinary Time 20	Pentecost 13
Aug. 21-27 — Proper 16, Ordinary Time 21	Pentecost 14
Aug. 28-Sept. 3 — Proper 17, Ordinary Time 22	Pentecost 15
Sept. 4-10 — Proper 18, Ordinary Time 23	Pentecost 16
Sept. 11-17 — Proper 19, Ordinary Time 24	Pentecost 17
Sept. 18-24 — Proper 20, Ordinary Time 25	Pentecost 18

Sept. 25-Oct. 1 — Proper 21, Ordinary Time 26	Pentecost 19
Oct. 2-8 — Proper 22, Ordinary Time 27	Pentecost 20
Oct. 9-15 — Proper 23, Ordinary Time 28	Pentecost 21
Oct. 16-22 — Proper 24, Ordinary Time 29	Pentecost 22
Oct. 23-29 — Proper 25, Ordinary Time 30	Pentecost 23
Oct. 30-Nov. 5 — Proper 26, Ordinary Time 31	Pentecost 24
Nov. 6-12 — Proper 27, Ordinary Time 32	Pentecost 25
Nov. 13-19 — Proper 28, Ordinary Time 33	Pentecost 26 Pentecost 27
Nov. 20-26 — Christ the King	Christ the King

Reformation Day (or last Sunday in October) is October 31 (Revised Common, Lutheran)

All Saints' Day (or first Sunday in November) is November 1 (Revised Common, Lutheran, Roman Catholic)

Books In This Cycle A Series

GOSPEL SET

It's News To Me! Messages Of Hope For Those Who Haven't Heard
Sermons For Advent/Christmas/Epiphany
Linda Schiphorst McCoy

Tears Of Sadness, Tears Of Gladness
Sermons For Lent/Easter
Albert G. Butzer, III

Pentecost Fire: Preaching Community In Seasons Of Change
Sermons For Sundays After Pentecost (First Third)
Schuyler Rhodes

Questions Of Faith
Sermons For Sundays After Pentecost (Middle Third)
Marilyn Saure Breckenridge

The Home Stretch: Matthew's Vision Of Servanthood In The End-Time
Sermons For Sundays After Pentecost (Last Third)
Mary Sue Dehmlow Dreier

FIRST LESSON SET

Long Time Coming!
Sermons For Advent/Christmas/Epiphany
Stephen M. Crotts

Restoring The Future
Sermons For Lent/Easter
Robert J. Elder

Formed By A Dream
Sermons For Sundays After Pentecost (First Third)
Kristin Borsgard Wee

Living On One Day's Rations
Sermons For Sundays After Pentecost (Middle Third)
Douglas B. Bailey

Let's Get Committed
Sermons For Sundays After Pentecost (Last Third)
Derl G. Keefer

SECOND LESSON SET
Holy E-Mail
Sermons For Advent/Christmas/Epiphany
Dallas A. Brauninger

Access To High Hope
Sermons For Lent/Easter
Harry N. Huxhold

Acting On The Absurd
Sermons For Sundays After Pentecost (First Third)
Gary L. Carver

A Call To Love
Sermons For Sundays After Pentecost (Middle Third)
Tom M. Garrison

Distinctively Different
Sermons For Sundays After Pentecost (Last Third)
Gary L. Carver

www.ingramcontent.com/pod-product-compliance
Lightning Source LLC
Chambersburg PA
CBHW072015060426
42446CB00043B/2551